Let's Camp!

Dona Herweck Rice

Publishing Credits

Rachelle Cracchiolo, M.S.Ed., *Publisher*
Conni Medina, M.A.Ed., *Managing Editor*
Nika Fabienke, Ed.D., *Content Director*
Véronique Bos, *Creative Director*
Shaun N. Bernadou, *Art Director*
Carol Huey-Gatewood, M.A.Ed., *Editor*
John Leach, *Assistant Editor*
Courtney Roberson, *Senior Graphic Designer*

Image Credits: All images from iStock and/or Shutterstock.

Teacher Created Materials
5301 Oceanus Drive
Huntington Beach, CA 92649-1030
www.tcmpub.com

ISBN 978-1-4938-9857-2

Printed in China
Nordica.082018.CA21800936

First, we  .

walked

Then, we  .

climbed

It was one long day.

First, we  .

rowed

Then, we  .

fished

It was one long day.

First, we  .

ate

Then, we  .

drank

It was one long day.

First, we  .

talked

Then, we  .

played

It was one long day.

First, we 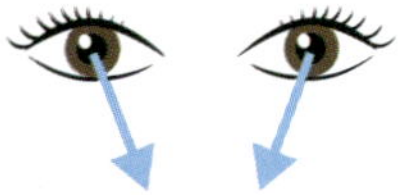 .

looked

Then, we  .

slept

It was one long day.

High-Frequency Words

New Words

day	first
long	one
then	we

Review Words

it	was